THE GREAT SCIENTISTS

CV RAMAN

Kavita Sharma and Aaliya Roy Kundal

Om KIDZ
An imprint of Om Books International

We all know plain water in a glass looks colourless. Then why does water in the sea look blue? Is it because sea reflects the blue colour of the sky? Not really. A great scientist called CV Raman explained why the sea appears blue.

Chandrashekhara Venkat Raman, or just Raman, was born on 7 November 1888 in Tiruchirappali, Madras Province (now called Tamil Nadu) in India. His father was a professor of physics and mathematics.

Raman was interested in science from an early age. As a very young child he would read the books his father had studied as a student. As he grew older, he began borrowing

mathematics and physics books from his father's college library. When he was just a teenager, Raman began reading the books his father had bought to do a master's degree in physics. He would spend a great part of his school vacations showing science experiments to his younger brothers and sisters.

A brilliant student, Raman completed his school at a young age, and graduated when he was just 16 years old!
He completed his master's degree in physics at just age 19!

Although Raman wanted to be a scientist, there were not many opportunities for science in India then. His family asked him to become an administrator, taking care of government affairs. He topped the competitive examination for the job and was posted in Calcutta (now Kolkata). Even with his job, Raman's deep interest in science continued. He spent his spare time in Calcutta working in the laboratories of the Indian Association for the Cultivation of Science. Stringed musical instruments and drums were his main area of scientific exploration.

The University of Calcutta was impressed by the scientific work Raman was doing. In 1917, they offered him the position of research professor. Raman, now 28 years old, happily took up the job because it meant he could give all his time to science. Besides doing research, he also gave lectures. He was a delightful speaker, and his students really enjoyed being in his class.

Raman's most famous discovery happened when he was on a voyage to Europe to attend the International Universities Congress of 1921. While on a ship in the Mediterranean sea, he saw the brilliant blue colour of the sea and became curious about it. He was so motivated that he began experimenting with a few simple instruments he had on board. Scientists at the time believed that the sea was blue because it reflected the sky. This belief was changed by Raman's discovery – called the Raman Effect.

Raman explained that the sea appears blue because water molecules in sea scatter the white light from the Sun. The light from the Sun looks white, but it is really made up of all the seven colours of the rainbow. When a beam of sunlight hits water particles, blue light is scattered more than the other colours and that is why the water appears blue.

The Raman Effect earned him respect worldwide. In 1929, the British Government knighted him for his work. He was now known as Sir CV Raman. In 1930, Raman became the first person from Asia to be awarded a Nobel Prize in any field of science. He was so sure he would win the prize that he booked his tickets to Sweden, where the awards are announced, four months before the winners were declared. He was right. He won the award and became the second Indian to do so!

Raman was made the Director of the prestigious Indian Institute of Science in Bangalore after his retirement from University of Calcutta (now Kolkata). In 1948, he set up the Raman Research Institute in Bangalore and continued his research.

After India's independence from British rule in 1947, the new government of free India appointed Raman as the first National Professor. He was awarded the Bharat Ratna, India's highest civilian award, in 1954. Raman also received the Lenin Peace Prize in 1957.

Raman continued his work at the Raman Research Institute until his death on 21 November 1970.

The Indian government announced 28 February as the National Science Day in his honour, because the famous Raman Effect was discovered on that day in the year 1928.

Raman's work has had a great influence on physics, and his curiosity about the world around him is inspiring for all.